Café Select

ABOUT THE ART

The images found in the galleries are the work of Miguel Condé and are reproduced with the kind permission of Serge Sorokko and Serge Sorokko Gallery:

> 55 Geary Street
> San Francisco, California 94108
> Tel: 415.421.7770

Condé's complex cultural heritage is reflected in his style and conceptual content. He deals with the absurd and enigmatic. He takes influence from the Byzantine artists, yet is deeply rooted in the political and social issues of our generation.

The works are available for purchase. If you are interested, please call the gallery or email as follows: ssrokko@aol.com

> www.sorokko.com

Café Select

W. M. Rivera

Poets' Choice Publishing

Copyright © 2016 Poets' Choice Publishing
All rights reserved
Printed in the United States of America

Consultant work:
www.WilliamMeredithFoundation.org

Bulk discounts available through www.Poets-Choice.com

Cover art: Miguel Condé
Artist's photo: Jorge Condé

Library of Congress Cataloging-in-Publication Data pending
ISBN 978-0-9972629-0-2

Poets' Choice Publishing
337 Kitemaug Road
Uncasville, CT 06382
Poets-Choice.com

Dedicated to my wife Sara

ACKNOWLEDGMENTS

The author is grateful to the editors of the following magazines where these poems originally appeared:

"Delmore Schwartz"; *California Quarterly, 2010*
"A Life"; *Poem of the Week, August 17, 2015.*
"Mistick Krewe of Comus"; *River Poets Journal, Autumn/Winter 2015.*
"Iceland and the Starfish"; *Broadkill River Review* 2015
"Free as a Bird"; *2River View,* 20:3, Spring 2016
"A Literal God"; *2River View,* 20:3, Spring 2016
"Arny"; *Broadkill River Review,* Fall 2016
"Generation Song"; *Broadkill River Review,* Fall 2016
"Manicured Cracks"; *Broadkill River Review,* Fall 2016
"The Drift of the Mississippi"; *Broadkill River Review,* Fall 2016
"Simonides"; *Broadkill River Review,* Fall 2016

The following poems originally appeared in *The Living Clock* (chapbook, Finishing Line Press, 2013):
"Let's Pretend," "The Living Clock," "The Scent of an Orange Peel"

......

I would like to thank my long-time friend and fellow artist, Miguel Condé for agreeing to publish a joint presentation of my poems and his images. Details on Miguel will be found toward the end of this volume. I also wish to express my appreciation to the editor, Richard Harteis, for the original idea of combining Miguel's artistry and mine, and for his editing, design and publication of this volume. Thanks to numerous colleagues and friends for their support during the development of this book, in particular, Carola Condé, Stephen Scott Whitaker, Greg McBride, Elisavietta Richie, and Ruoyi (Gale) Gao who encouraged me in my creative work.

"... precision is not the opposite of mystery."

Louise Glück, *Proofs and Theories*

CONTENTS

Acknowledgments /vi
Introduction by Stephen Scott Whitaker /ix

I. Lunch with O'Hara

Art's Kick /3
Prelude /4
Lunch with O'Hara /5
After the Poetry Reading /6
Disembarking the Drunken Boat /7
Manicured Cracks /8
A Peacock on Marlborough Way /9
In the High-Pitched Dark /10
120 mph /11
Why Make Believe? /12

Gallery I: Paintings /13

II. Carpe Diem in Retrospect

Coffee at Le Select /31
Tarantulas /32
Mistick Krewe of Comus /33
A Nearby Hotel /34
Winter Is a Shivering Girl /35
A Perfect Treasure /36
Death Brings Her Back /37
The Scent of an Orange Peel /38
'Le Vert Galant' at the Yard Sale /39
If Just for Coffee /40
The Puzzling Chemistry of Desire /41
Passing Fancies /42

Gallery II: Watercolors /43

III. Pascal in Mexico

Mary Meanders Home /59
Pascal in Mexico /60
The Magic Trickster /61

Free as a Bird? /62
Delmore Schwartz /63
Hotel Picture Window /64
Bewick's Wren /65
Her Punishment /66
Grace /67
Blank Paper Thighs /68
Fickle Queue /69
Arny /70
Emperor Qin /71
A Literal God /72

Gallery III: Drawings /73

IV. The Placement of Forks

The Placement of Forks II /99
Ode on a Thundermug /100
The Drift of the Mississippi /101
The Boy down the Block /102
A Long-Stemmed Rose /103
Yesteryear Ripples /104
Carpe Diem in Retrospect /105
For Granted /106
A Pike Rose /107
Nude no. 139 /108
Prick the Heart /109
The Origin of the World Close Up /110
Out of the Shadows /111
Valery, I Disagree /112
Naked at the Met /113
Such a Nice Day /114
Rain /115
Accelerated Death Benefits /116
Simonides of Ceos /117
Generation Song /118

***

About the Artist /121
About the Author /123

INTRODUCTION

By Stephen Scott Whitaker

"Truth, a dominatrix/asserting love is all..." W.M. Rivera writes in "Prelude," one of the opening poems in the book you are holding. Truth can be pleasurable, and painful all at the same time, like love and sex. This exploration of truth and love as double edged sword runs through *Cafe Select.* Rivera's poems are lusty gems, there's a fighting spirit, and a wise one at work in these poems, sometimes wrestling with itself, other times wrestling with the great spiritual chink in our armor, other people and their influence upon us.

Rivera kinks it up in *Cafe*, and I'm not just talking about sado-masochistic sex, or a lusty young couple in heat, the lines of these poems screw into each other creating a dense tough lyricism that is coupled with gritty reality:

> these 'sperm on the wing.'
> Most won't make it.
> Some end up in luxuriating in Rimbaud's bathtub boat
> on a pond in Tuileries Gardens. Some labor
> growing pains on death-row's dry concrete.
>
> In suburbia most land on fertile ground.
> Even the run-amucks multiply in manicured cracks.

Rivera's describing dandelions seeding into air in "Manicured Cracks," how most won't make it, that the seeds of the weed, the most iconic of spring youth images, faces a fate like all of us. They might live on to flower again, or they won't. As human counterparts, many of us will die along the way, and often the worst of us, the weeds, thrive. What I like is the music in Rivera's poems. The alliterative urge, the hard consonant sounds, very much like later Seamus Heaney, acting like sharp edges to confine and crib the lines and feet.

Poetry and art are created by privilege, and these poems are unabashed at their modernist raiment made possible by a privileged life. Paris is both the geographical and figurative heart of the book. Paris, the literal city, and Paris the epitome of culture. Rivera is at home on both fronts, and relies on music to drive his poetry forward; the imagery, well that's extra sauce for the pudding, and whether he's referring to the city of lights, to art in a gallery, or to ancient Occidental poem, it doesn't matter. For Rivera their origins are the same. The urge to create, to be reborn.

In many of these poems, Rivera explores the passive rot of suburban life, the almost sadistic impulses to live a passive life, to view other lives unfolding in pain. Our modern world demands that we watch. Our TV remotes and mobile electronic devices demand our attention. And the opposing forces of light and creation? Too often left to the side.

We are transitory beings, Rivera knows, and though we play pretend at all sorts of notions, the one constant in life is the novelty of love. A gorgeous face in the crowd, a quiet cafe on the corner, a woman's clothes hugging her curves, these matter. And art matters, too. And Rivera explores art of all kinds, paying homage to Rimbaud, and even Baudelaire, the painter Miguel Conde, among others. To fight valiantly against boredom, and rot, by wielding art and in love can lead to one's rebirth. And Rivera is not just speaking of the contemporary impulse, he's exploring the history of making a life out of art, the choice of making a life out of making art. Is there a better way to while away the hours? Making art and consuming art is as valid and as important as laying brick, and quite fun, too. Reading Rivera, one can sense the smile as he writes. He's having a blast.

Café Select is as much about love as anything else, and sex, and desire's agelessness. This "itch" defines our desires, a woman's backside as she walks away, an undergrad's décolletage peeking out of a sweater. Desire, after all, is one way to pass time, and as transformative as art, and as fleeting as a gallery walk. Love can make anyone a fool. It's the oldest trope, our need to fall in love, our hungry desire, our private lusts; perhaps the loudest noise of all.

Rivera's poems tease us, not in a mischievous way either, but in an honest, earnest way, as if he is saying, what do I know of our "diminishment?" He is, like us dear reader, willing to wonder if age and loss illuminate our spirit, our inner lives. "Why else invent these reveries?" Like a painter, Rivera captures hundreds of details in a chaotic busy scene and renders the busy and chaotic scene serenely, effortlessly, a work that somehow appears to us not as many scenes, but as one large cohesive glimpse at humanity.

Rivera's poems rattle the senses. His poems compose order from chaos, and his eye is ever looking. With a Romantic's ear for lyricism Rivera's poems explore mankind's highs and lows, our lust for beauty, and the folly of love.

I

Lunch with O'Hara

Art's Kick

You judge this another nothing as you
slum through 'poems of the day,' hoping
for art's kick to engage your senses
as you flip by, looking for
an unusual mix, say, condensed milk
with bitter herbs, eager for one neuron in
one hundred billion to make a connection
between silences, even if it's not much,
a little noise to trigger a nod, a yes,
which routs your inner critic, your endless
wish for stanzas that twist, go on,
kick butt, something quick, but ages long,
to find yourself, condensed in sweet song,
or bitter insight, just for kicks!

Prelude

Once I revered Greek gods, Zeus
lusting between thighs, morphing
to shun Hera's watchful eye.

Call it myth what I believed
pulling the shades to hide and scratch
walls for immortality.

What was it years ago?
trapped me in this mimicry, swept along
yet stuck, glue-trapped on a dusty floor,

raised on commandments, stone tablets,
street smarts, learning to discover
Beauty is not Truth but make-believe,

and *Truth* a dominatrix demanding
love is all and death but prelude.

Lunch with O'Hara

O'Hara thought we didn't do much in the 20th century
but "fuck and think." We thought about fucking, for sure.
I devoured *Shunga*, eating *the other* up in my head,
tipping the velvet, yodeling crudities and smelt salmon.

Hope is always a hot tomato. Or, too hard.   N*o hope now*;
some say; the 21st century is already fucked.
It's time to bite our tongues: go under, pack up. No hope
to escape from wars to Mars either. Still,

Don't despair, drowning is worse. Sex is all; O'Hara,
I agree, it's what we do. Eight billion this century! Wow.
That's fucking! Now it's time for lunch. There's a thought.

Disembarking the Drunken Boat

Rimbaud, darling of poets
called on us to be visionaries!

Disembarking his "Drunken Boat," he sailed
trade winds, steered toward guns, gruesome
voyages destined for massacre,
waived the unreal for lucre's appeal.

Ignore the blood sea's skull and bone,
he sets our sails afloat, coddles our ego-whore.
Who cares he fed war lords and braved the heat
to deal in death, our darling boy, poets' pet.

Manicured Cracks

Watch the dandelions in summer flourish, their seeds in the air,
watch how they unfold tiny umbrellas in the volatile wind,
the ribcages stretch open to catch currents. The seed pods
on their haphazard odyssey: up and off,
these 'sperm on the wing.'

Most won't make it.
Some end up in thoughts of Rimbaud's bathtub boat
on a pond in Tuileries Gardens. Some labor in
growing pains on death-row's dry concrete.

In suburbia most land on fertile ground.
Even the run-amucks multiply in manicured cracks.

After the Poetry Reading

Everybody stands, relieved. She's not
at ease, shy, on her own
wave-length, the choice not taken, those
urges to run off, but then, quick hide.
Love, who loves it anymore? She smiles,
a smile of disappearing, finally at home,
she pets her ancient dog. The call to go out
dissolves, and she retreats into dreams
infallible, safe under quilted covers,
complete inside herself again, her thighs
well known. Her hand between,
her sighs bring peace. A distant touch once
infused with sunburst power, still there, what
groping poets once claimed prepared to die for.

A Peacock on Marlborough Way

Bombs over Palmira, sky-jacking
in Cyprus, on the sidewalk
my friend calls me to walk faster,
stretch my legs. And off
we go. Exciting? No. But wow!
a peacock on Marlborough Way...
disappearing into the brush. Unusual, yes,
where lawns are trimmed in fantasy—
wind-animated geese, ducks in a row,
yellow dolls with nails and fluff.

He didn't fly. Ducked
into an open backyard.
This peacock on Marlborough Way.
We lost him.

And what about the screams of wars and immigrants drowning,
events wishy-washy in my head. Nothing to write about there,
only this peacock, making the heart thump extra,
escalating breath. Animating. Blotting out wars.
Energizing our walk, that day on Marlborough Way.

In the High-Pitched Dark

Cajoled into a ghetto movie house,
porno extreme. As we enter her scream
ricochets off the halls,
stiffens the audience, eager
for the next episode, and here it is:
a cat thrown on a teenage back.

Edgy chuckles in the cinema's dim light recall
neighborhood kids torching a cardboard box,
giggling as the mouse inside runs wild.
Shrieking in delight, the lust to witness what
wrecks humanity and titillates the brain.

The rush of blood that stirs sadistic art,
the fascination with another's pain,
the exquisite shiver in the high-pitched dark,
wanting to hold, or be held, helpless.

120 MPH

120 mph, New Orleans to Tampa.
Highway-10 truckers blink me on.
Why is it some survive, that sudden skid,
life's goodbye? Others speed by
hell's gates, as if that place were still off limits.
Many want to go on, and don't.
I prop them up in words, ones I hardly thought
about, and place them on cirrus clouds,
close to the almighty urge to fly, I ask them all
the same question: 'Why?' Is it 'luck?' Or
anthropomorphic gods gritting teeth,
but looking the other way? Or, like so many
"why's" ended with 'OK, what comes next?'

Back then, I raced to feel the sweat, that
near-death quiver. Unfazed by the ambulance, twirling
lights, the sirens, far-off thoughts of swerving too late. I came close
that day, eager already to tell how it felt, near-death.

Why Make Believe?

Tu Fu once asked, "What for?"
Why write of fashions, war!
To be remembered?

Yet Stephen Crane hired men to read his work
conspicuously on elevated Chicago trains!
He said, "*Why wait till you're dead!*"

To huge surprise, Rimbaud heaved overboard
his boat full of illuminations, escaped poetry
for business, running guns at sea.
Why make believe?!

Yet observe how Hokusai
in his print of a fisherman's wife, lust-aching,
arching up as a wide-eyed octopus slurps between
her lush thighs, finds ecstasy.

Gallery I

Paintings

FOTÓGRAFO

OIL ON CANVAS
43" X 39"
2013
SIGNED

UNTITLED

OIL ON CANVAS
52" x 71"
2013
SIGNED

UNTITLED

OIL ON CANVAS
41" X 37"
1988
SIGNED

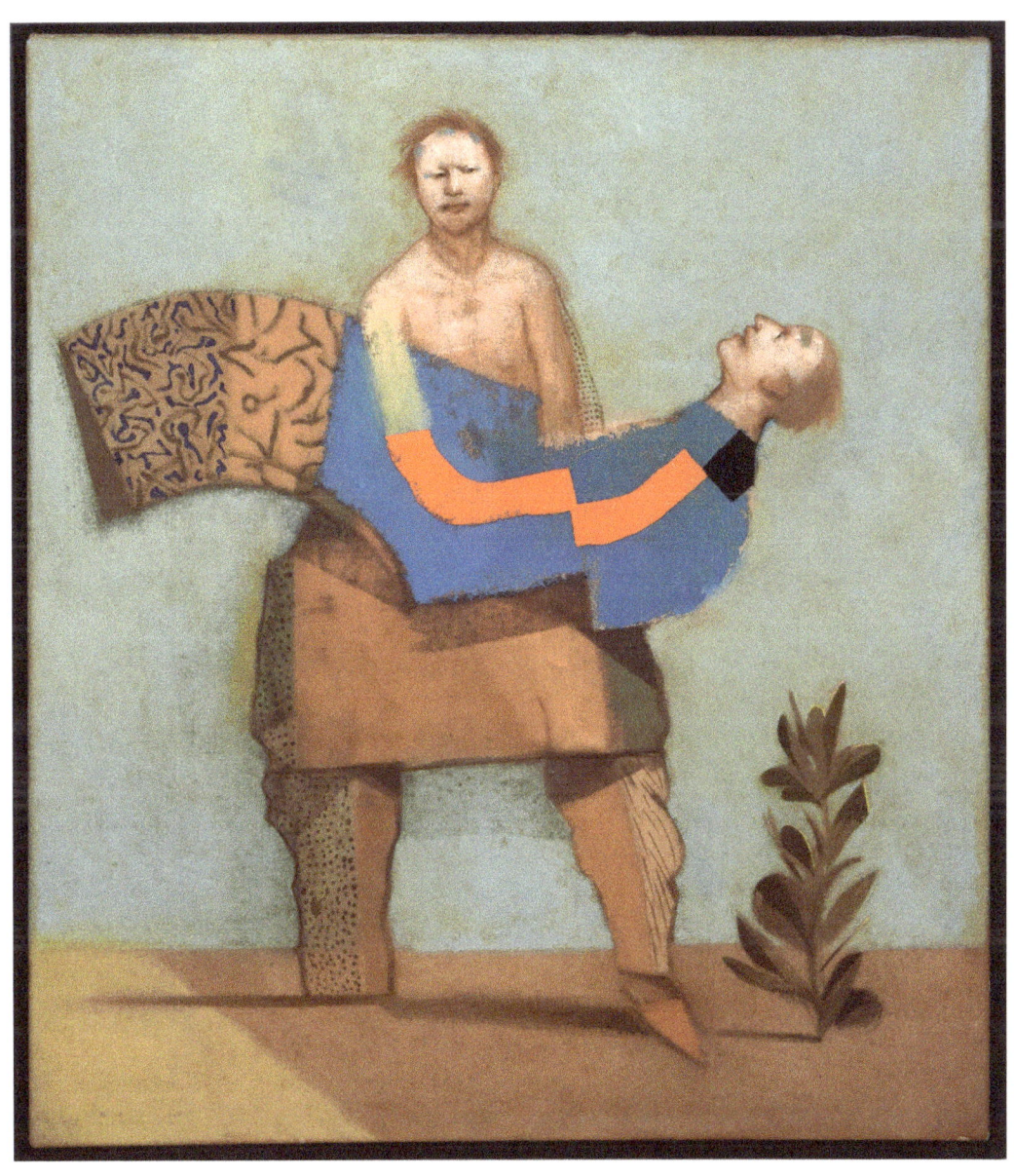

Untitled

Oil on canvas
40" x 36"
1988/2010
signed

Untitled

Oil on canvas
47" x 36"
2013
signed

UNTITLED

OIL ON CANVAS
41" X 37"
1975/2011
SIGNED

UNTITLED

OIL ON CANVAS
77" X 51"
2011
SIGNED

II

Carpe Diem in Retrospect

Coffee at Le Select

Sipping coffee at Le Select, across from the Dome
and the new squeekly-clean facade of La Coupole,
in Montparnasse, I watch them pass, al fresco,
objects of desire.

The eyes, the waist. She has the appeal of Cranach's Eve,
Ingres' Odalisque. My mind's a bedroom of reclining nudes.

What adventure! That one, her hair falling back.
her ankles two daggers in my on-looker eyes.

I pledge my heart to passers-by, one three cups away
inspires trajectories, al fresco,
object of desire.

Tarantulas

Speeding across Texas, bent for Mexico to mend
a marriage, my stomach in my throat,
I see one long consuming darkness in the desert distance,
no oil spill gloom, but hairy legs blanketing the highway,
tarantulas seeking females, miles of black brown bodies,
packed in eight-'fingered' *urges*.

Sliding on flattened silk, I brake toward the shoulder,
stop to look closer, their bodies along the ditch
deep with wriggling up on either side. I watch them creep
underneath the car. On tiptoe wheels, for miles I crawl
that highway's length. They crawl across my mind,
specks of anxiety, shadows of lust.

The Mistick Krewe of Comus

New Orleans Mardi-Gras parades began mid-19th century, formally launched with the Krewe of Comus.

Mules pulled the floats back then.
The Krewe members in bright-white facemasks,
dressed like sheiks, blow kisses
to women shrieking for the 'throws' they fling across the crowds,
strands of beads, fistfuls of doubloons.
The women blow kisses back at the Krewe's members.

Mardi Gras kids snatch at the green, gold, purple, yelling,
"Throw me somethin', Mista," taking chances reaching
beneath each float's curtained under-wheels. Gaslight
spilling from flambeaux for made-in-Japan trinkets.

The street's a trampoline; the crowd like Masai dancers
springing up in air tirelessly for keepsakes, jammed in between
cheek-hugs and howls. Beings squeezed against plump derrieres

trumps sanity. Hands grab at whatever's thrown, the litany of me
let loose full force, joy screaming toward what floats away.

A Nearby Hotel

That long-ago Rome, midnight, lamplight,
Italian, blonde, 20, soliciting.
I thanked her for asking, helped me
decide I'd spend un-budgeted *lira*
on gifts for the girl back home.

'Drop-dead gorgeous,' that golden-haired
street goddess! Don't fault me if I fantasize.

It's a blue story: a girl who wants you
and you're far away in the future. It's not just
her beauty inhabits the mind,
but the stories you can't truthfully tell
how we frolicked that night in a nearby hotel.

Winter Is a Shivering Girl

*"Winter," a sculpture by Houdon (1741-1828)
in the Metropolitan Museum of Art in New York.*

'Winter' is a shivering girl.
A shawl, that's all, shapes her body,
her bottom bare.
How did she get there wrapped in nothing
but a shawl? Poverty, you think. Locked out?
I imagine her pushed into the cold, naked,
the wind cutting to the bone, only a shawl pulled tight
over her head, her behind exposed,
her body bent, her tempestuous story
congealed in pain that never thaws,
raw winter once the hard door shuts.

A Perfect Treasure

I found her rapt in a magazine
on an outskirts bus to center Paris. I was a tourist,
museum bound. She shared a photo framing
an Afghan treasure, once stolen, carried place to place,
a treasure: flowing skirt, tight waist, a noticeable backside crease.

She spoke in slow French for me,
how the stolen treasure exposes *a new opening into Asian mystery.*
A perfect piece, a 1st century river goddess,
recovered intact inside a sunken ship off Indonesia.

We ambled along the Seine, her boyfriend killed in war's affairs.
I asked her *to kiss*, though the word I used meant *to fuck*.
She corrected my French. Laughing later, the hunger
hard in her taut curves, stirrings deep as wreckage
in a tip-toe upstairs hotel.

Death Brings Her Back

Death brings her back,
her crotch squeezed in her short shorts,
gave me the ouch when mine tightened.
One night, that's the sum of it.
But the news brings her back
in a line of early whims, and me her next,
both licking lips; me, biting mine.
Our satisfied itch, scratched and moisturized.

What's left is her shape, her face dim.
Her curves in short shorts.
Nobody to me now, but not nothing then. The news
brings her back. A 'whim' and a 'next' never die.

The Scent of an Orange Peel

For Katharine (1932-2015)

Random thoughts, our rubbing noses; planting seed.
Then the icepick pains chip away. Nothing lasts,
Ha Jin in his *Ways of Talking* knows, after existential grief
we long for things beautiful, *"even hailstones in the strawberry fields."*

But that grief is spent. *Spent* grief is different,
an unburdening, whinnying the wheat.
No more promises to keep, even this one, to remember you,
breathing in the odor of an orange peel.

'Le Vert Galant' at the Yard Sale

The French King Henri IV (1553 – 1610), a great womanizer, known as "Le Vert Galant."

Ambling among throw-away treasures,
maybe this or that...
Yard sales awash with women.
His wife says he has a Casanova Complex.

> One brunette, reaching down, his eyes up
> her skirt, peeps as her hand ties her sneakers.

'Le Vert Gallant,' I call him King Henry,
high on his horse, overlooking Pont Neuf, as if
casting for lovers along the Seine's drift.

> One blonde squats full view; her maxi
> mid-thigh. Big sigh. Eyes

this way and that, yards awash with treasure,
he rides from sale to small pickings: an African mask,
mysteries under wraps, bric-a-brac.

If Just for Coffee

I discard urgencies on the calendar,
sneak a preview of the light flowing
through the window slats, remove
earlier objectives from the future,
ignore the sun-up's insistences. This morning

I am a happy man. Swept up in the flesh,
the new day's newfound focus, I ignore
imagination's web of lost images,
reshape the edges of chaos. It's a perfect
today, the kind of day I've been waiting for,

knowing you, not knowing you, only
knowing you're coming, if just for coffee.

The Puzzling Chemistry of Desire

Love lures on, lasts and outlasts
who comes and goes. Once
gone, the tangible ghost of it
is missed, not the Eve or Steve who shared
with you love's puzzling chemistry,
but the thing itself, the intangible allure, that

beaver under her skirt,
his cock a bird with wings.

Passing Fancies

"My desire has ambitions on them all." Ovid's Amores, 2.4.

"You can't have them all," my son grumbles.

"Yeats never stopped looking," I snap back.
If I were a gynecologist, I'd still enjoy
fashion's pink, the wink… high heels.

> I love the make-believe;
> tightened thighs passing by.

"You can't have 'em all," he mutters.

Delighting in places I've never been,
I eye them clicking in their catwalk spikes,
their printed pantyhose. Behold!

old images, passing fancies. I have ambitions on them all,
Tantalus must be my brother. I live on tenterhooks.
I stretch for one, just missed another, passing fancies.

Gallery II

Watercolors

UNTITLED (DIPTYCH)

PEN & INK, WATERCOLOR AND
GOUACHE ON PAPER
80" x 60"
2011
SIGNED

UNTITLED

PEN & INK, WATERCOLOR AND
GOUACHE ON PAPER
40" X 60"
2012
SIGNED

Untitled

Pen & ink, watercolor and
gouache on paper
60" x 40"
2011
signed

UNTITLED

WATERCOLOR ON PAPER
15" X 14"
2012/2014
SIGNED

UNTITLED

WATERCOLOR ON PAPER
10" X 9"
1996
SIGNED

III

Pascal in Mexico

Mary Meanders Home

After Todros Abulafia, 13th century

Dragging her hem, her dress covered with mud,
Mary ambles home, slows to see the Roman soldier
staring, her staring back.

Did she decide to differ?
Take a stance against tradition? Or was she lured

by dazzle, that Roman afternoon,
the walls tumbling down? Her legs clutched round

his head, crying 'Lord!' – Thus
the godhead nucleus forms; the frog kicks
in baptismal time.

The newborn have their noses held,
dunked in the living waters
some claim her son walked upon,
wet with the why of what survives.

Pascal in Mexico

> *...todavía hay tiempo para desconfiar y no arrepentirse,"*
> heard on the street in Mexico, D.F.
> (trans.: 'there is still time to question your belief and not repent')

I thought God was history. But in the streets I watch
earnest hands wave new-born belief, their latest truth.
One voice sings an ancient tune, a voice unquestioning,
unrestrained conviction, God's own.

Then a hawk dove into the overflow of what I heard;
I quote, "There's time to question your belief
and not repent," convinced he knows the truth,
his nitty-gritty pin-points the other side.

The streets expand with attitudes. A lyric view
I hear, horns in. She says: "Ponder how you'd describe
the indescribable, formlessness from which forms flow."
Her gesture touches my blind side. Words are tricky.

'God this! 'God that.' Each time I say it, hear it,
I'm 'surprised. A habit like sugar,
this babble on a vapor trail.

The Magic Trickster

Black holes in the universe confirm
the reality of becoming nothing, which changes
everything, flattens the concept of our atoms ongoing
in another form yet still in this same world,
whether nearby or far flung, a part of what is
supposed to last evermore in our floating gravity.

But now, that genteel notion is kaput,
new knowledge of reality, reality
with *nothing* added,— a foreign gravity grabs
what passes by its black-hole path.

How conceptualize our galaxy as *something for dinner!*
our evolution, the nature of things learned for *nothing*?
dragged into a black hole, zapped! The 'magic trickster'
nowhere to be seen! Nor hide nor hair of us!

Free as a Bird?

How hard in soil and sky birds work!
At least the caged bird eats, albeit at the cager's will.
It's archaic: *free as a bird*.

Even their mating games arise from compulsion,
and their fights?...to gain a dying worm, a slug,
remnants from the garbage truck. Even the stars
in sparkling speed shine toward certain fixity.

Of course the peaches bought today, hard rocks,
might still take off with auks next week
and skim north waters... white-breasted on tuxedo wings.

We hunt, peck, rap, swing blue pen poems
the color of flight suddenly flashing the wind, hovering
over sustenance to suit our mood. Always hungry.

Hotel Picture Window

I met a woman who told me she wrote
to twist events, snigger, scribble pain.
How once she scratched in wet concrete
her heart-throb's name, wobbly firm. When love
hardened the indelible remained, underfoot.

Later, she framed her world to win
quick fame, spun make-believed memories,
her black moods served to entertain,
or goad in others fear as when
light flickers and the reaper skirts the room.

How one time, she felt she touched
the Moon in La Paz. "Huge," she said,
"level with the hotel picture-window,
firmer than names carved in stone."

Bewick's Wren

White eyebrow
stripes, multi-tasking,
maybe out for a date, flicking its tail at a feckless worm,
a Bewick's Wren … a ripple, an air-burst
unsettling the leaves. Too soon. And me, maybe you too

thinking to catch the exact moment…that thought
before the flash of feathers, the white eyebrows,
already gone.

Delmore Schwartz

At the end of life, a lone wolf
in Times-Square's wilderness,
gutterized, crawling under
garnered rags, bedbugs in his nights, no recourse

on 42nd street: "Escape!" the bottle cries.
In flight, his images bend light bulbs
frozen in art's ice. He liquefies life's chains,
the city's rush, scrimmaging for gain;

in his veins Bohème sings the stars asleep
against the blur of noisy bars.
Only his companions remain: dog, bear,
dark alleys, dead ends, the sky's edge

where he stumbles off. The apple, fig, whatever
they offered him, the taste was hell.

Her Punishment

She crawls out the window,
three flights up, dark, shapeless.

Night knows no dawn when misery leads on.

She squeezes toward the ledge,
her exit, now slumps over the roof's edge,
looks down toward...
what is it? Nothingness?

I stand beside her, stink in a splattered heap.
A suicide at my feet. Why remember,
her imagined *must-have-been*?
I see her sprawled body
like St. Andrews' in an X.

For now, against her will or wish
I frame this as her final punishment:
words meant to make her share
once more her lasting memory.

Grace

In memory of Grace Granger, doll and puppet maker.

Dear Grace,
Mother had me call you Aunt when you weren't.
I loved you in the painless ways children do.
You fabricated dolls drawn from dreams and the famous:
Marie Laveau wild dancing at fiery Pontchartrain,
gris-gris nights, voodoo highs. I wish I could recall
your gumbo girls, each stuffed on shelves, in corners,
unmoved the day you fell from cancer down the stairs.

"Ma chère," my mother cried, that day they took you off
still clutching your favorite white-winged Angel Doll.
Steeped in faith and scared you had not paid enough
to be redeemed, you gave
your tightly held one million saved to save
your soul—seeking comfort through dark space,
your fear. I think of Hieronymus Bosch
whose hells some churches post along the walls
to cause the flock to pause and to give. You gave your all.
'Why not!' you said, your family gone, husband dead. Yet,
when the nuns shaved your head and dumped you
in a metal bed, it seemed a bitter pill—told to chant Hail Mary's
to alleviate the pain. You, maker of famous.
faces for Maison Blanche department stores. You worried
about your puppets unprotected, home staring at the wall;
hug Angel Doll, watch white-wings fly by, starched
headdresses outside the inhospitable door.

Blank Paper Thighs

On his newly painted white walls, with black
felt-tip, I scrawled: *peddling dairy-air*, and
a leaf wiggles in no-breeze. If inscribed on biscuits,
Han-shan knew homeless dogs wouldn't deign to nibble.

My German host sang *fame cantar*, off-key, *a cappella*;
called hi song *in-deli-bil-ity*. I guess he knew
he'd paint over it next day, my scrawled 'great poem',
our drunken howls. That night writing on the wall

we prove we were living, pretended to immortality.
I wrote her name, then smudged it out. You know
how love leads on to love, I only know her name
meant life itself, one time ago.

I dig up her photos, each an instant's fixity. And this
frames us, my friend and I, the same-faced characters
we've become yet changed. It is abstract what's real.

Being in a picture where you were *somebody else*,
younger, still remembering who you meant to be
back then, what's not, inevitables you couldn't avoid:
 a gun up your nose, war, Icarus handing by a limb.
Her far-off flesh become blank-paper thighs.

Fickle Queue

A two-lane by-way, through oak and maple.
A line of cars behind me,
wipers rubbing away rain's blur,
rush bumper close.

I slow to stop, blinkers on,
block the road, ignore the hail of hateful honks,
step out to pick it up: a speckled high-domed
box turtle waddling toward the yellow line.

Drivers impatient in metallic, painted shells,
wait, restless, watch us, turtle and me,
cross this busy by-way. At last,
exhale, their heads half out

in the mizzling wet, they wave,
hearts happy now, honks on hold.

Arny

For Arnold Kaltinick (1940-1981).

I knocked the angel-shaped magnet off the fridge
by chance and with it a piece of cloth from
a clothing store named "Arny's," the same name
as my dead buddy, my 'younger brother,' I called him...
died years ago. Unexpected remembrance makes me shiver—
the magnet falling, with it the piece of cloth.

We met in Acapulco, then kept meeting—tourists in Guanajuato,
out of the blue in New York, Paris.

Before his posthumous PhD on socialist mayors in American cities,
I thought it was a bad joke this business he started
just before the end, his selling firewood, as cancer
burned him up. He wrote me only: "The clinic's clean."

Times like this, I wish I were religious and believed
we'd meet again, in some incredible city of lights, reach out,
grip hands, wrestle.

Emperor Qin

*Qin Shi Huang, born Ying Zheng also known as
King Zheng of Qin (259-210 B.C.)*

His terra-cotta soldiers, their chariots, the horses
standing steady underground, ready for the quest
not to discover, not for gold, but to enter heaven.
A dream-march, Emperor Qin devised in detail—
his army parading him through fancied royal gates,
displaying the munitions of a man with dignity.

Qin conceived a throne, high on his horse, the highest,
no other aim than to arrive, his new venue
to show off victories and again to rule with dead-
weight hands. He meant to dazzle, excavated
earth to plant his troupes, readied the monumental trek,
not just to prove his own 'undying' but to be revered

trumpeted by celestial bands. Deluded? Still
his name remains, the quest and the march to get there.

A Literal God

A literal god is best, the Methodists
taught me. The whale did swallow Jonah.
'Believe, and you will arise.' I imagine
summer steam in the air, absorbed as rain
kids stamp their feet in.

It makes little difference
what I thought, or think. I see
St. Christopher hold hands with Fatima.
Sure, it was a jumble, a jungle, a jigsaw, Jesus,
Siddhartha, Mohamed, Zeus.

I grew to love Akhenaton's insistence on one god,
the Sun, Aten, a literal god, neither stone nor burning bush,
or any other imitation of invisibles meant to occupy
the center of the universe. The Sun,

champion of the way things are seen. It shines
so brightly when it shines, what else is there to know?

Gallery III

Drawings

UNTITLED

PEN & INK ON PAPER
5" x 6"
1980
SIGNED

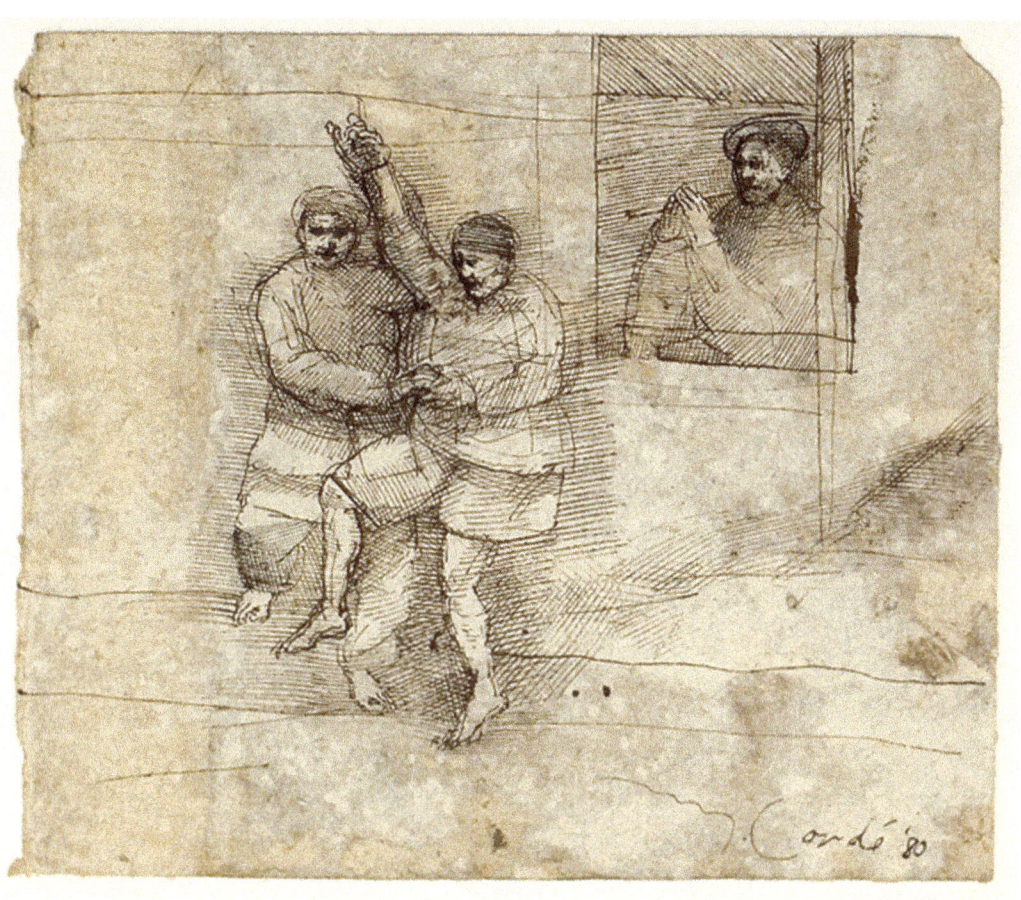

UNTITLED

PEN & INK ON PAPER
14" x 16"
1976
SIGNED

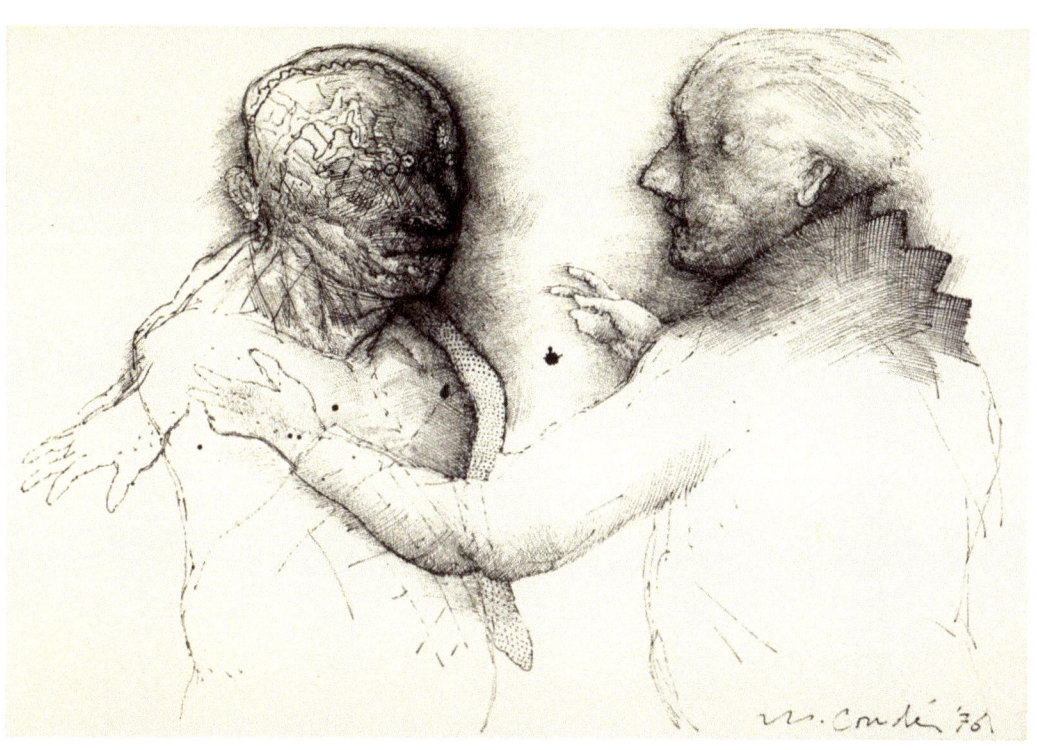

Untitled

Pen & ink on paper
12" x 8"
1981
signed

UNTITLED

PEN & INK ON PAPER
8" x 6"
1980
SIGNED

Untitled

Pen & ink on paper
8" x 6"
1980
signed

Untitled

Pen & ink and gouache
on parchment
16" x 10"
2002/3
signed

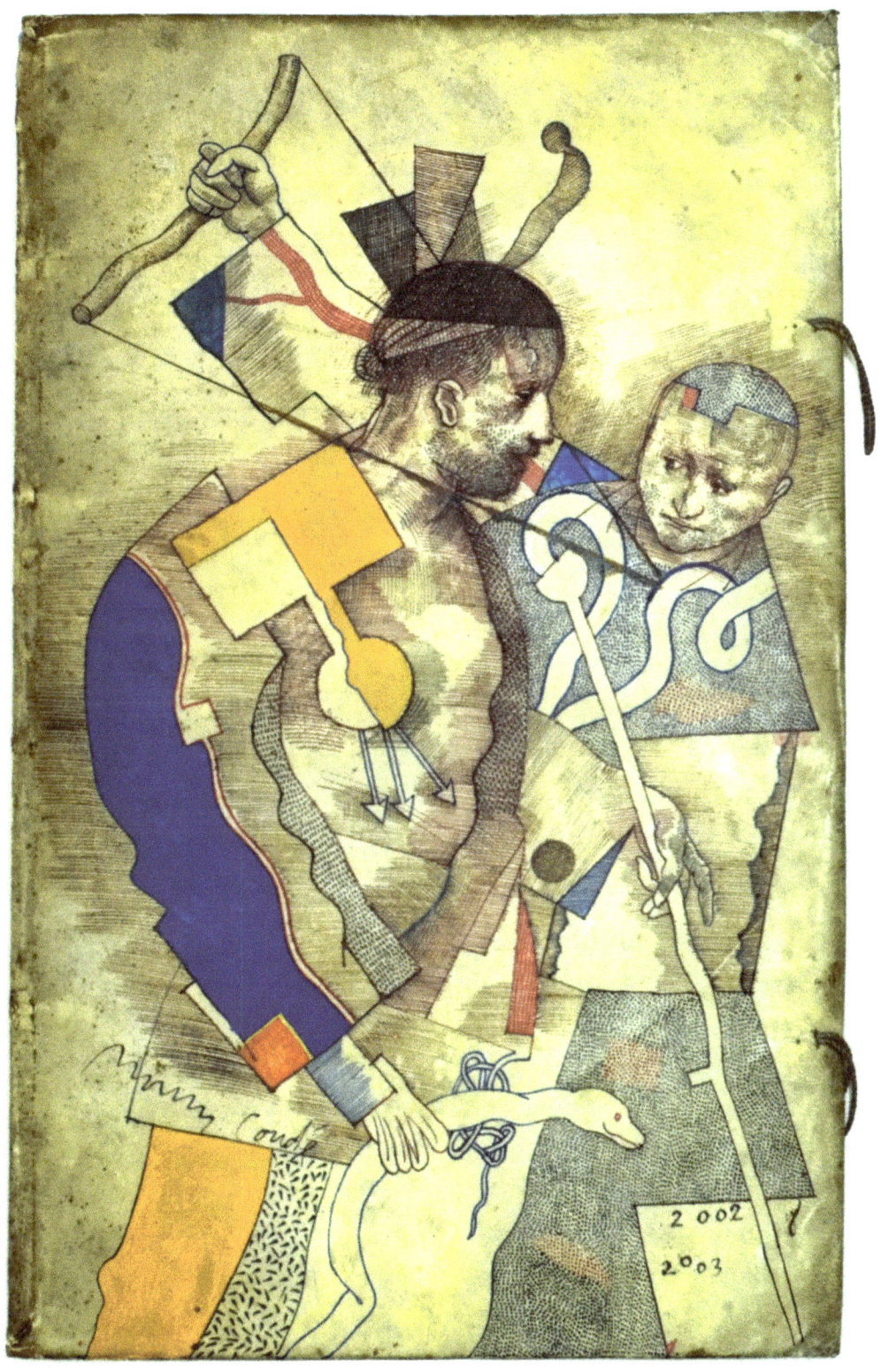

UNTITLED

INK & WASH ON BOOKCOVER
16" X 10"
2005
SIGNED

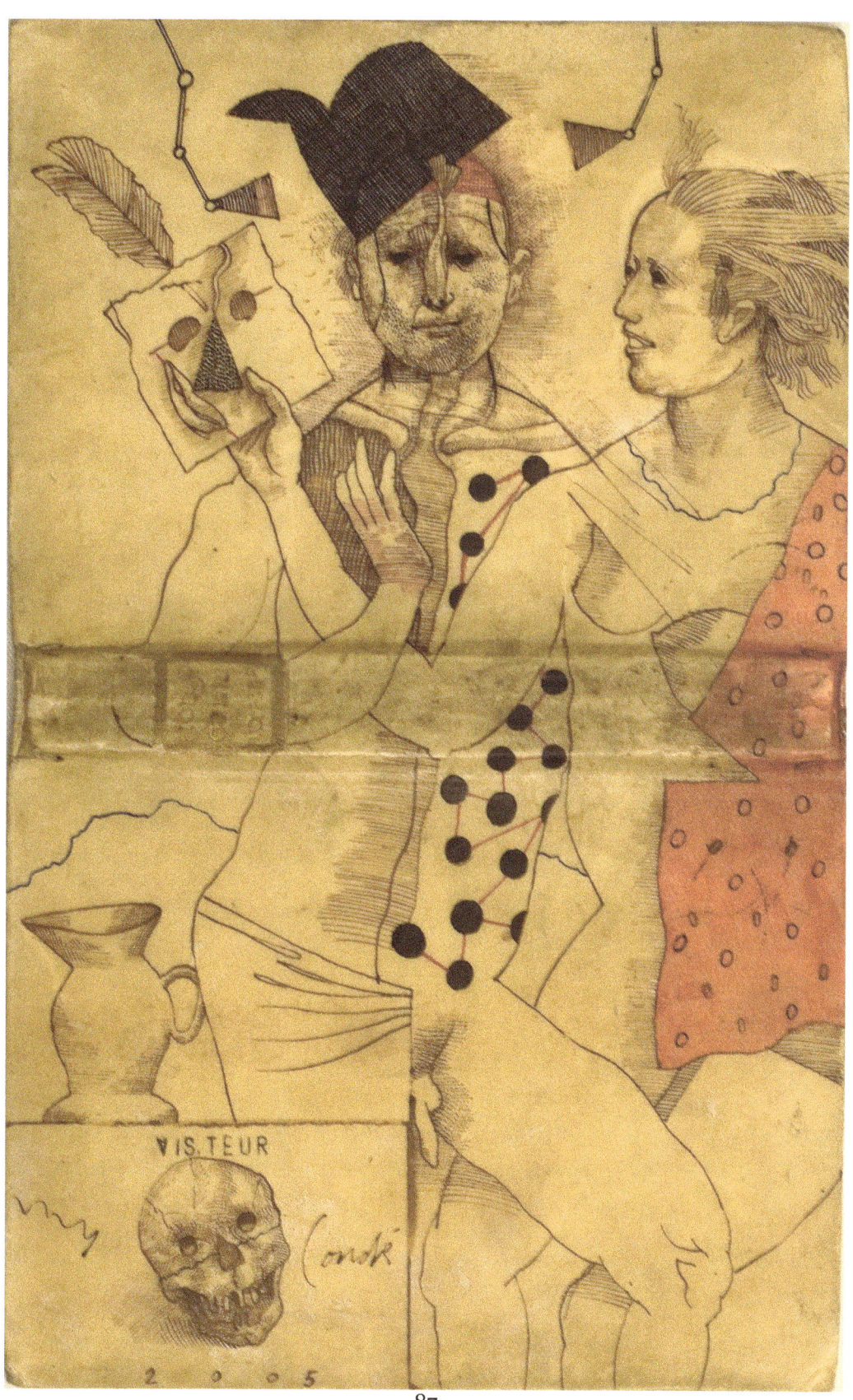

UNTITLED

INK ON BOOKCOVER
18" X 13"
2009
SIGNED

UNTITLED

INK ON BOOKCOVER
18" x 13"
2009
SIGNED

UNTITLED

INK ON BOOKCOVER
14" X 13"
2014
SIGNED

UNTITLED

INK ON BOOKCOVER
20" X 14"
2007
SIGNED

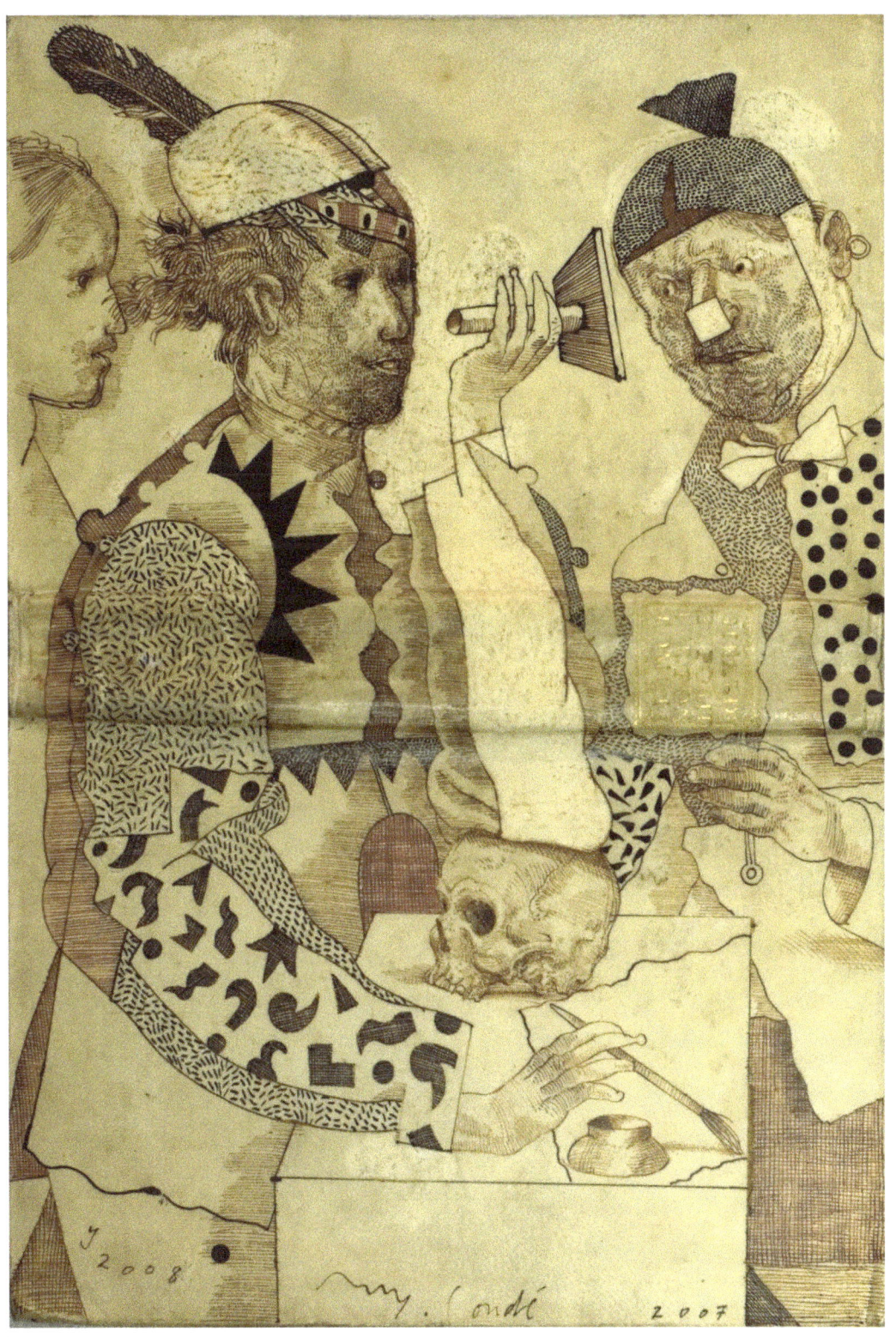

IV

The Placement of Forks

The Placement of Forks, II
A poem for my grandmother

When in the kitchen, my grandmother made it clear
she'd cook the perch I caught, if scaled and insides cleaned.
Over lunch that day, she pointedly arranged the silverware;
taught me to set table. Meanwhile, she extoled our heritage,
went on about our family's standing in the community
back then. The Civil War ruined them. But '"one good thing',"
she owned this double-backed camel house. When one
thing broke, go to the other side, she said.

Like me, that day, the cats and dogs were antsy as she laid out
victuals, waiting, impatient. They knew, especially the cats
she would soon hand out bowls and saucers, talk to them,
out in the alley about their blue-blood, Egyptian and Siamese. But
before that, "Don't go in the house." And she meant it. I saw her
boot one cat, screeching, clawing air.

Her stories of Scottish industry, rich in the 19th-century
up until the 1860's War. On and on like exposure to cannon fire
I soon grew deaf about the family history! Eager to grow
'up-up-and away'. What did they matter,
ancestral portraits framed in gold-leaf!

Rooted roots in ashes; my own in air ... Death means nothing
to her now. The streets still littered with summer drunks,
the drool of destiny. Staunch love she taught,
things far off and the placement of forks.

Ode to a Thundermug

> *"So what seems to you to be a barber's basin seems to me to be Mambrino's helmet..."*
>
>   Don Quixote to Sancho Panza

Once a helmet of Quixote's Moorish king,
the target where the knightly arrow aimed,
the handle of an unremembered dream.

As water lies quiescent mounting toward
its rapid fall, half conscious not to make
much noise, or miss, a small ghost rises up
in childhood two-step unsteadiness.

Tonight I half reach down as if to raise
that water pistol, wanting not to wake her,
then a room away, my grandmother, my Mambrino's
Queen, breathing toward the void. Nightly,

life's fiction accumulates, small urgencies
relieved, a stream of vanishing keepsakes, shadow
sounds, outpourings for a bedside Thundermug.

The Drift of the Mississippi

*The Mississippi River is steadily shifting towards the
Atchafalaya River channel, disastrous for port New Orleans.*

New Orleans hugs the water. Its grip is loosening ...
the Mississippi is running off with French Quarter land.
Lace waves unraveling in the wind, wind
away from British Petroleum's overlay. What's coming
changes everything: Highlife in a new land.
Will the city tire of what's been
sold down her river, westered away
from her long-time Quarters,
drawn to the current's oleaginous beads.

Massive yet elegant in her slow hurry,
she leans into the drift of it.
The evening Sun goes down,
already a gurgling sound.

The Boy down the Block
Remembering Calliope Street in New Orleans

I watch Bobby the boy down the block
become *femme* as Douglas the boy
across the street in his mother's,
the charwoman's just-cleaned classrooms
sodomizes him on a ping-pong table, back
before the school became left-over bricks.

Bobby in bathrooms down at the Y
fellates young members, relishes behinds.
Ah poetry, the bottom of *refine*.

Douglas moved away. Bobby grew curvy,
joined the Navy. Belatedly I wave them both
goodbye, applaud their dogged dance,
holding on to one another, a little *to-do*
between streets Saint Charles and Camp.

A Long-Stemmed Rose

Non fui, fui, non sum, non curo.

I've been here before, a boomerang
at memory's door, shadows in back
of l'Eglise de Saint-Germain-des-Près.

Two benches, four people, noon.
A long-stemmed rose on the outdoor
bust of Apollinaire, a fat-faced remake

staring off into what's no more space
for him to write in, a blunt gaze
already worn, positioned where

there is no fear of death because
there is no more death for him, yet he wrote
as if he were aware his past were living, as it is.

As if, he felt the pain of shrapnel in his dome,
still dying to upend the world, burn down the Louvre,
as if poetry were made more real in the face

of his figures caligrammes to flaunt old forms.
As if his Polish name were not: Wilhelm Albert
Wlodzimierz Apolinary Kostrowicki, just

Apollinaire. As if the rose gave off a touch of red.
As if he rose above the seasons wear. Remote as
pigeons peck the lawn for serendipities.

Yesterday Ripples
For Sara, 28 February 2015

Where are the travels to Sidi Bou Said?
the fountains of Rome? Arenal?

You drink the *non-potabile* in Trevi, wet to your thighs.
In Tunis, the evenings westering, sky flush with swallows.

Or how forget that wild white horse at the slope up
from Arenal, lava, easing toward us, alive, smoking ash.

Of course, it wasn't all pennies in fountains, artists over-
looking the Mediterranean, iguana screams, lava-love,

but prickly hair-pin curves, our constant braking,
hairpin curves we combed through each other's knotted hair.

I mix bad with *good and best* to make this credible waffle.
Taste the spoon again. Those cayenne days.

And now, the echoing sounds
only the Earth hears,
trees taking root.

Carpe Diem in Retrospect

Eyes in the City of Light turn on. No
promises to un-keep, no late laments; no guilt
came and went. Who knows what might have been,
what ending best becomes?

Flowers fastidiously handpicked, fixed in long hair.
No lust too long, no trip too far:
fucking was everything.

What's there to know? Notches
in a counting game, learning time's tomorrow
stumbles on today, this *carpe diem* introspect,
a dated theme of 'grab-it-now'
in retrospect.

For Granted

I once saw a hypnotist hand
empty eye-glass frames to hypnotized students,
said to see through clothes. And they did,
proving Errol Morris, *believing is seeing*.

Not-seeing is also believing: knowledge seen
as what you want to happen—longer life perhaps,
that brain particle primed to say yes
to incredible promise.

Early pastimes, bubbles in hidden
eight-page 'bible-books,' that cartoon world's
*raunchy rumps half-mast, schlongs and yonis thrust
into incredible clouds about to burst, pots boiling over.*

"This is this, and that is that;" my grandson at 3 decided
words are wishes, to confirm, bring back—your subject
not just a printed object, a real child,
in grandmother's kitchen, licking the spoon,
taking the cake for granted.

A Pike Rose

Cat-fishermen chuckled at the spoon-feathered lure
I arched into the River weeds. One guffawed. Until

a pike rose, gulped the feathered spoon, and stood up
glittering, a spangled dancer, making their eyes leap,

mine most—casting out into the unlikely. Like now,
sharing this lyric of that day:

A pike, caught, not without a struggle. Fan tailing,
flashing. A high-table day. Walking on air.

A kid-fisherman's peak day. Scaling pike for dinner.
For days I hovered over myself, searching for wings.

The saying goes "who laughs last, laughs best."
Too much light in my eye to see the moral!

Nude no. 139

An Irving Penn photo, at the Metropolitan Museum of Art

I am caught up in a crowd closing in on a gelatin
silver print, a photo of a woman, a somewhat heavy woman
in a 'lounge' pose for the camera. She displays
what the suited man next to me calls "thunder thighs."

The crowd turns her over in its mind, Irving Penn's
Nude 139. Like me, I presume we see
the body is the thing— the belly, one breast, one thigh,
no arms or feet in view, elbows underneath. Seems
completely at ease. Her fleshy torso folds in on itself.

The small crowd's eyes are drawn, *more like slide*,
toward the print's center, the slight-
ly exposed pubic hairs, the shadow of her vulva, and also
that one prominent puddled breast.

Nude 139 is a Greenwich morning-after thrown-together
beauty off-hand, yet organized. The model
is not *La Grande Odalisque*, lives closer to home.
No harem whore, yet ready to be stirred up,
her body odors and perfume, waiting for you
to voyage in her continents.

Prick the Heart
For Ruoyi

You say you wasted your life.
Few will remember what you put together,
tore apart, perfect afternoons, urgent
embraces, romps on the lush earth.

Too soon the treasured leaf's a skeleton of veins.
Love, it never was for keeps: hurried promises,
lifelong lament.

Who knows what might have been,
what ending best? A little while
bright flowers last – desire, despair,
I know. Both blur the view, prick the heart.

'The Origin of the World' Close Up

Courbet, L'origine du Monde, 1865

I examine the vagina in a close-up photo,
flaps and hood, such a modest proposal!
A bump above a closure into one
we came out of, going into, spelunking for what
we cannot find outside the cave.

I examine the idea of *it,* how
it lifts the spirit, as skirts fly up and the libido
links legs with the limbic at the mere seeming sight,
the thing itself, a bushy blur swimmers shave
the bald soft flesh, the waxed

landing strips. I examine its brashness in a video,
a woman in golden dress exhibits herself before
Courbet's *L'Origine du monde.* Plopped on the floor,
legs splayed, her pubics unshaven,
dark with arrogance and disorder. And I, like
a hummingbird hovering, dipping into the taste
of unmistakable life, find nothing lessens its allure.

Out of the Shadows

Out of the shadows
fireflies pop up, there and over
there. The woods blank to bright.

Watching their impulsive starts,
abortive stops, I fancy it is *moss-code* rap,
lights on, off, blank to bright.

To be old is a weird gift, taking time
seriously, not as a series of events,
degrees, deeds, but nights peppered blank to bright.

How gentle their distraction from the dark, their sparks
diverting moments from blank to bright.

Valery, I Disagree

You wrote, "Poems are never completed,
they are only abandoned." Think children who leave,
don't come back, stray dogs loosed at the edge of town
to die, but don't. It is true

some come back, like the patio pigeons in Coyoacán
I tricked with crumbs scattered beneath a propped-up
cardboard box. Hauled them off to Chapultepec Park.
And that was that, I thought, but they came cooing back.

What bothers is the silence once poems are deserted.
Insights overlooked. Regrets for what I missed
or made in haste, or wasted. Gone but left behind,
those irritating bits of blubbering, itches
scratched not close enough to bleed. You are right,
I apologize: homing pigeons, whatever reminds me
what I did or didn't do, what doesn't go away.

Naked at the Met

Apollo's lament at losing Daphne.
Metropolitan Museum of Art.

I nearly caught her, but she closed me off.
She'd rather be a tree, she screamed, then morphed
her arms to branches, fingers full of leaves.

All because I said Love's little boy played
with toys better meant for war, but found
his bow and arrows more lethal than I thought.

He pierced me with the sharpest pain, then ran
her off. Now seems a lark, my unrequited lust
and her quick arching rough with hate

into harsh bark. It's true I mainly coveted her
moist velvet prize—my hunger's monologue,
what women crave but wait for what their mind

dictates. Matters little now, my fate. Except lost
love and limp indignity, fixed naked at the Met.

Such a Nice Day

I don't like the thought of it either,
the thought of being dead. Dying's the operative word.
The thought is obsessive. No turning it off.

And it's such a nice day! Don't worry,
her's is no gloomy tune to back-up the record.
Rather the sound of silver-bells and a nursery rhyme
about 'one damn petunia,' graciously keeps tuning in,
keeps in mind a basic destination.

Still, life can be depressive in its repetition,
going nowhere or rather round, like that:
the birds are gone, then back. You're up; you're not.
No 'click' to shut the scratchy record off.

Whines on, and on. Such a nice day!

Rain

Month of May 2016, P.G. County, MD

I think of James Wright lying in his hammock,
viewing a field of sunlight, cowbells, a chicken hawk,
waxing ironic. But this rain, relentless,
undermines the *hubris*-tall trees.
One oak-autocrat topples over on a nearby house.
The water rising, I contemplate relocation.

It "Never stops!' my neighbors curse,
furious with their fear of flooding. I think
Gilgamesh and the Flood of Noah. The fear is
flood's waste! This evening between light
and dark, I'm OK with butterflies and irony,
but stuck in this place divining basement funk.

Accelerated Death Benefits

This is new. You can append a rider to your policy,
pony-express the benefits. No matter the unknown hovers
over every clause, smiling at death between the lines.
As always the errant road is fixed and accidental.

I'm going as fast as predictable. Yes, please
accelerate my death benefits. I know you won't like it,
you other dears, who'll get less. Still, damn it! It
quickens what I get to spend while I waste away.

At the Honda Dealership where I sit, reading insurance
brochures, acceleration is the norm. Service staff clip,
staple start to finish. I smirk at 'accelerated benefits,'
watch the clock slow towards my assigned wait time
when suspense is a loud speaker and life just the facts.

Simonides of Ceos

> *'Poems on the page that's where their strength lies, infused from ink to eye, no eardrum second-hand communication.'*
> Simonides of Ceos (556–468 BC)

His Victory poems celebrate what he expected of a poem, prowess,
revelation. He contends poems are best on the page.
"Infused from ink to eye, that's where their strength lies."

Not all agree: the auditory came before text, no separation between
poet and poem; a special class of speech with singer and the song.

But Simonides saw a play as fabrication, not the understanding
source inside you. He argued the poem is in-between
the page and you. No rapping on the podium. Reading is
first-hand connection. Even the voice, practiced aloud,
to validate cadence, distracts.

An Open Reader added to this argument. "You know," she said,
"*reading out loud to an audience isn't like reading it to yourself.*"

For Simonides, poetry's personal, seeing for yourself by yourself.
No interpretive voice, only how you imagine
the wren, swift from the branch, leaves shaken. Innuendos.
Music direct from ink to eye.

Generation Song

This past fall's leaves,
the wind helping them fall
finally, flutter down.

I think of connections:
70% of my DNA can be found in a slug.
The leaves could be ancestors.
Few remain. My family tree is but a pencil sketch
in grandmother's King James version of "The Holy Bible."
But there's a difference, the remote dead in a book
and the dead once known in life.
My reach for the remote is half-hearted; but it's all part
of a losing generations song. I hear its silence

in those hanging-on sere leaves, giving up one by one
as if never capable of ever being anywhere
but in the moment, letting go.

ABOUT THE ARTIST

Born 1939, Pittsburgh, Pennsylvania.

Miguel Condé is a Mexican figurative painter, draftsman, and etcher. Born in Pittsburgh, he split his childhood with his father in Mexico and mother in the United States. He currently lives and works between Madrid and Sitges, Spain.

Miguel Condé studied anatomy with Stephen Rogers Peck in New York and etching techniques in Stanley William Hayter's Atelier 17 in Paris. His colorful paintings and drawings are speckled with leitmotifs and *dramatis personae*: characters that instill a visual language that Condé uses to poetically express his relationship with art history and the world around him.

Condé's work is in major collections around the world, including the Museum of Modern Art, New York, the Art Institute of Chicago, the Brooklyn Museum, New York, the Bibliothèque Nacional de España, Madrid, and the Smithsonian Museum, Washington, D.C. He is a recipient of a Guggenheim Latin American Fellowship.

ABOUT THE AUTHOR

W. M. (William McLeod) Rivera is a retired agricultural educator. His academic background includes a B.A. from the University of North Carolina, M.A from The American University in Washington, D.C, and Ph.D. from Syracuse.

He taught agricultural extension and development at the University of Maryland (UMCP) from 1981-2009. After retiring from UMCP, he has dedicated his energies to writing poetry. Three collections of his poems have been published, and he was a nominee for the Pushcart Prize in 2012.

Insights and experience from his birthplace, New Orleans, his career specialties and travel working in over 15 countries, provide much of the context for his poems. "Le Select," the Montparnasse café in Paris, provides the imaginary background from which he reviews his experiences and life's ventures.

He and Miguel Condé met in Mexico in the late 1950s. Both have Mexican fathers and American mothers. Both love art. Their pathways have continued to come together, as do the poems and images in this book.

www.ingramcontent.com/pod-product-compliance
Lightning Source LLC
Chambersburg PA
CBHW061928290426
44113CB00024B/2848